The Extraordinary
Spirit Sightings
of an Ordinary
Surrey Lady

The Extraordinary Spirit Sightings of an Ordinary Surrey Lady

Marianne Green

Winchester, UK
Washington, USA

First published by Sixth Books, 2013
Sixth Books is an imprint of John Hunt Publishing Ltd., Laurel House, Station Approach,
Alresford, Hants, SO24 9JH, UK
office1@jhpbooks.net
www.johnhuntpublishing.com
www.6th-books.com

For distributor details and how to order please visit the 'Ordering' section on our website.

Text copyright: Marianne Green 2012

ISBN: 978 1 78099 813 8

A CIP catalogue record for this book is available from the British Library.

Design: Stuart Davies

Printed and bound by CPI Group (UK) Ltd, Croydon, CR0 4YY

We operate a distinctive and ethical publishing philosophy in all
areas of our business, from our global network of authors to
production and worldwide distribution.

CONTENTS

The Early Years and Beyond   1

Spiritual Encounters, a Psychic Attachment and
    the House of Ill-Luck   18

Our Auras, a Personal Psychic Attack
and Further Spirit Contact   31

An Outstanding Angel Sighting, Déjà Vu Evidence of
    Animal Spirits and a Pathologist's Spiritual Sighting   45

The Never Failing Love, Protection and Care of the
    Spiritual and Angelic Realms   55

Chapter One

The Early Years and Beyond

I was born in a quiet Surrey suburb in a small semi-detached cottage situated in a leafy green lane. Large purple and dark pink rhododendron bushes flanked both the garden and the edges of the woodland opposite our cottage. According to some of the other local residents, there were some old undetonated World War II bombs buried deep within the woodlands and I can remember at times police cars travelling up and down the lane with loudspeakers attached instructing all the residents to stay indoors as a possible bomb was being investigated. Thankfully, none to my knowledge were ever discovered! We did however come across grass snakes, many varieties of insects and also birds' nests, and some of the pale blue and white coloured eggs could sometimes be spotted in our back garden, courtesy of my two brothers, who used to endeavour to watch curiously for any signs of the eggs hatching.

There was a country feel to our back garden, with apple and pear trees scattered about amidst blackberry and redcurrant bushes, along with masses of sweet smelling pink, white and maroon coloured sweet peas. At the far end of the garden was a rickety old wooden fence with holes underneath which separated us from a neighbour's smallholding. I can remember on many occasions, small pink squealing pigs escaping into our garden, racing at top speed with my family and the neighbours following in hot pursuit trying to get hold of them!

Our cottage was always a lively place with my parents, my two brothers, me and my grandmother living there. There appeared to be a lot of people at times coming to visit my grandmother, Amelia, as she was known to have the power to foretell the future with her incredible intuition. I can clearly remember her with her long, flowing, dark hair, sometimes twisted up into a pleat at the back of her head, and deep, dark, brown eyes which always appeared to be darting here, there and everywhere.

She was half French, and both grandparents on her mother's side had come from just outside Paris. Apparently, her father had owned several coffeehouses dotted around the London area, but unfortunately in his later years had taken to gambling away many of his prized shops! She always seemed to carry around a large pack of playing cards with her, and there was frequently a huge pot of tea on the go, together with several brightly coloured china cups and saucers at the ready for her visitors.

After her guests had had their tea, Amelia would ask her visitors if they had any questions they would like to be answered. The cups would then be turned in an anti-clockwise direction three times, and my grandmother would then quickly turn them upside down so that she could proceed to give a reading from the grouts of tea leaves left in the cups. She used to always say that the tea leaf grout patterns left near to the cup handle represented the client sitting in front of her. The patterns of grout to the left of the cup handle represented their past; the grout patterns on the right of the cup handle represented the client's present and future life. The cup's rim grout patterns showed their very immediate present i.e. the next one to two days. The tea leaf grout patterns in the middle of the cup referred to the following two weeks, and those lower down the cup showed the next three to four weeks. Apparently, only "China" tea was used specifically for this purpose.

Later, my grandmother would always produce her special

pack of playing cards, which included the usual suits of diamonds, hearts, clubs and spades. After shuffling the card pack with great speed, she would then ask her client to also shuffle the pack, after which my grandmother laid the cards out on our large wooden dining table and proceeded to arrange them in certain mystical patterns and give her client an even further in-depth insight of their life. Apparently, her visitors all left our cottage afterwards in a far happier frame of mind than when they first arrived, having drunk not only a cup of the very best China tea, but having also had an accurate confirmation of their past, present and future lives predicted via the tea leaf grout patterns, and also the playing cards. Not forgetting, most fortuitously, having received the benefit of my grandmother's uncannily accurate intuition.

I can also remember my late Auntie Winn (my grandmother Amelia's elder daughter) telling me how she had worked in a solicitor's office in the City of London for many years, travelling by train to and from Walton-on-Thames, Surrey to Waterloo station, London and then onwards to the City of London. However, on one particular occasion, after getting herself ready early one weekday morning to embark on her usual rail journey to London, her mother (my grandmother) strongly urged her not to travel that particular morning as she had a truly black feeling that something terrible was going to happen. My Auntie Winn, thankfully, heeded her warning, as tragically on that particular morning her usual train was involved in a serious rail crash and there had been several fatalities. (I also believe that my grandmother had frantically endeavoured to contact British Rail earlier that morning with her warning.)

I firmly believe that we are all part of the unstoppable Nature Kingdom and that our own Earthly existence would appear to follow in a similar pattern, which I often describe as:

Our spring time (our 'blossoming' cycle)
Our summer time (our 'blooming' cycle)
Our autumn time (our 'converting' cycle)
Our winter time (our 'preparing' cycle, for our return to the Earth's soil)

Only then to triumphantly re-emerge the following springtime (or 'blossoming cycle') to follow the same growth pattern.

I would like to mention my incredibly wise father, William John. He had always had a harsh life path to tread, ever since his childhood years when he was born the eldest of six male children in a small cottage in Hook, Surrey. Sadly, his mother passed away at the early age of 41 years through sheer hard work and exhaustion, and so he helped raise his five younger brothers. As finances were tight his father, Jessie Green, worked long hours on the railways.

He also had to bring some money into the household budget at the tender age of eleven years by caddying at a local golf course. He was always determined to pull himself up by his bootstraps and spent many of his late teenage years and early twenties educating himself and also studying to become a heating engineer. He was always a strong, positive man and took responsibility in his stride, always offering to help those in need. He was always acutely aware of what was occurring not only just in his personal world, but also in all aspects of our Earth plane, as well as the Universe and beyond. After much studying and deep thought, he held an unshakeable belief that we humans were all part of the Kingdom of Nature, and that our lifecycles were constantly being illuminated, extinguished, and later miraculously re-ignited. He also felt that there were many other dimensions within the Universe, often quoting the biblical phrase "In my father's house there are many mansions," which he must have thought had some relevance in this respect.

I remember vividly, on many occasions, my father gathering the whole family around our large oval shaped dark Oak table in our front parlour. He then proceeded to lay out small, white cardboard squares with black alphabetical letters on them in a circular pattern, and then place a down-turned empty long stemmed wine glass in the middle. We were then instructed to all place our index fingers on the glass, and after a few minutes of silence he would then ask if there was anyone from another dimension, or the spiritual realm who would like to come through and be with us. (I know that there may be those of you reading this who have a differing viewpoint about this activity, but it was always carried out with our total belief in the spiritual after-life dimension and that a spirit would only come through if they wanted to speak with us, and always we would all feel very humble and honoured to be in their presence.)

The glass, to our amazement, would sometimes slowly tilt from side to side, and then move around to the various alpha-betical letters. On many occasions it spelled out the name of the spiritual energy present in the room, often imparting information regarding their name while they were living on our Earth plane, and details of what they did for a living and the place, all of which was utterly fascinating to us. Sometimes the spirit would inform us that he/she had lived here many centuries ago, and then go on to describe the events that had actually occurred during that particular time. On one occasion the spiritual energy present told us, by moving the glass very slowly to each letter, that he was a very old soul who had lived on Earth during the 14th – 15th centuries and had been a highwayman who had held up coaches and held the rich occupants to ransom. Another spirit informed us that he had lived and worked in the 17th century at a tavern in London and very falteringly described his life there at the time, sleeping on straw matting on the tavern floor, and suchlike.

There was one particular occasion when the entity guiding the glass had some information specifically for me. At that time I was only in my late teens, and was sitting next to my younger brother. I was informed that the person who would eventually become my life partner would originate from the York area of England and also that I would have three children. Strangely enough, several years later, all of this information actually materialised, but alas not for me, but for my younger brother sitting, as mentioned, next to me. So, disappointingly, it appeared to have been some sort of a spiritual mix-up, or perhaps just the entity playing games?

I attended many psychic talks, demonstrations, workshops and development circles during my younger years and often my late mother, Marjorie May (who was extremely intuitive herself), accompanied me. Two outstanding psychic mediums whom we met at that time were Joseph Benjamin and Doris Collins. Mr Benjamin had a marvellous sense of humour, with a twinkle in his deep, brown eyes and my late mother and I visited him at his London home several times.

On one of these occasions we were waiting to see him in a small downstairs room of the house when the door suddenly opened and in walked a very famous American male film star of the day. We just stared at him in a rather star-struck fashion, too speechless for words. He just smiled broadly at us and appeared to be visibly taken with my mother (whom, I should add, was an extremely attractive woman at that time). On another occasion, we visited the famous Doris Collins at her home in Richmond, Surrey. She would often mention her good friends 'The Goons' (a well-known group of comedians) and also the late, great Frankie Howard. She was a warm, entertaining medium of the day, and we felt so lucky to have met her.

Our mind, I personally believe, has three states of consciousness, i.e. the conscious rational mind – the logical, every day, intellectual part which looks after all our bodily functions. The powerful subconscious mind which records and memorises every event that has happened to us throughout, not just our present life, but also other incarnations that we have lived through. The subconscious can be programmed and will respond accordingly. In fact, even some of our illnesses develop firstly in the subconscious mind by our very own thought power, as thought is another very powerful energy. When we think thoughts of happiness, love and success you would be amazed at how life can change dramatically for the better. Lastly, and most importantly, there is our higher self which is the pure spiritual part of us where our spirit (or soul) is housed.

There are various meditation techniques, some of which are as follows:

1　The observation of your breath a few times i.e. breathing gently through your nose, via your diaphragm, and holding for a few seconds before exhaling slowly.
2　Candle flame – focusing on the golden flame and imagining it entering your heart with each breath, thereby bringing great tranquillity.
3　A guided meditation, usually by way of listening to a spiritual teacher's voice and calming angelic background music.
4　A transcendental meditation when we can repeat, or chant, a particular word or phrase, or even hum a sound, thereby making a vibration which can also help us in attuning to our physic and creative sides.

Through meditation, we can alter our mind state and can

actually bring to the fore several varying states, enabling us to make contact with the spirit world more easily. These mind states are:

1 The alpha state occurs with deep relaxation and can help us to attune to our creative and psychic sides. Energy waves, namely Schumann waves (which are the fluctuations of the Earth's electro-magnetic energy field) synchronise precisely with our psychic and healing mind states.
2 The delta state occurs when we are in a deep sleep.
3 The theta state is when we are asleep, and is connected also to our creative and psychic sides; also this particular mind state links to inducing what is termed a trance state.
4 The beta state occurs when we are being active.
5 The gamma state is the quickest of the five wavebands and is to do with all our complex thoughts.

Once the alpha state has been reached and we have meditated, we can then psychically use either a mixture of what is known as the Clair skills, or just one of these gifts, which are listed as follows:

Clairvoyance	-	clear seeing
Clairaudience	-	clear hearing
Clairsentience	-	clear feeling
Clairtangency	-	clear touching, sensing through touch
Clairgustance	-	clear tasting, sensing through taste
Clairscent	-	clear smelling, sensing through smell

I always endeavour to reach the alpha state before giving a psychic reading and always ask my Spirit Guide and Guardian Angel for guidance with the reading as well as using a mixture of the above Clair skills.

I would like, if I may, to tell you about my mother, Marjorie May, who was not only extremely intuitive, but also very intelligent with a quick wit and sense of fun. She had been born in London, the middle child of three girls and the family having been fortunate to come from what was termed then 'good stock'. They had all received a good education and had lived a comfortable lifestyle, living in a three-storey property in Kingston-upon-Thames, Surrey. My mother was always smartly dressed, without a hair out of place, and because of her educational opportunities, she was able to land some very good positions of work, including in a solicitor's office where she would often be present at court when there was a client to represent. This was something of a feat in what was a man's world at that time.

My mother tragically suffered with Alzheimer's disease for nearly twelve years in the later stages of her life. I won't dwell on the suffering that she so bravely endured, but would just like to say that my mother deserved a medal for her bravery and non-complaining (as, I am sure, like many other sufferers of this terrible disease).

My late father loyally looked after her every single day at home, but sadly she had to eventually go into 24 hour care at Ottershaw Hospital in Surrey where both my father and I visited her daily. Sometimes he would visit my mother twice a day, even pedalling the long distance to the hospital in order to try and save a little on petrol money. He was fully retired at that time and financial circumstances had of course altered. I can remember very vividly one particular evening that will remain in my memory for ever, which was when we had returned home later than usual after visiting my mother in hospital. It was a bitterly cold evening and on entering the house my father went to every room and turned all the electric and gas fires up to their maximum heat (we did not have central heating at that time).

Approximately an hour later we were sitting in our cosy living room having supper when suddenly the whole room went icy cold. We were startled to find that the heat from the fires had reduced to barely anything at all. We then ran all over the house, only to discover the same thing in every room. Obviously we both were feeling completely puzzled by what had happened. We started to shiver and had to pace about just to try and keep warm. At that point my father, who appeared to be deep in thought, looked straight at me and speaking in a sombre tone stated, 'I think this is spirit trying to warn us that your mother will be taken tonight.' His words were confirmed when just before 5.30 am we had a call from the hospital advising us to return. My father and I literally just jumped into the car and drove as fast as possible, luckily 'de-thawing' on the way, as the car warmed up quickly. However, after having driven for approximately 25 minutes, the car strangely went freezing cold and at that precise moment we both instinctively knew that my mother had passed into the spirit world. Sadly, upon our arrival, this indeed was the case and the exact time of her passing had been 5.55 am. (We later learnt that an icy cold atmosphere is a sign of spirit being close.) This was yet another amazing spirit warning.

As the years passed, I began to give psychic readings both to friends and family and to people from all walks of life. A remarkably unusual reading was when I arranged to meet a young Yorkshire lady in the Portobello Road area of London. The client arrived complete with her gorgeous little dark haired baby girl who had the most enormous dark brown eyes I had even seen.

We went to what appeared to be a Moroccan type of coffee bar which had plush, dark brown leather sofas everywhere, stained wooden floors and leopard skin rugs scattered about and there were brightly coloured paintings depicting blue sea, people and flowers. We found a small wooden Oak table near the entrance and after a cup of frothy coffee the psychic reading commenced. However, an old-fashioned brown and white coloured jukebox standing in the corner of the coffee bar suddenly started up. It began to blast out Elvis Presley records, at which point the little girl sitting in her pushchair next to us started to howl!

Amidst all this commotion, the psychic reading strangely continued, bringing both insight and anticipation for the young lady client. Her baby girl then started to smile shyly through her beautiful dark fringed eyes, especially when my coloured tarot cards were laid out horizontally across the wooden table, at which point the little girl attempted to pick up and play with her own handpicked 'personal' cards. Some of the Elvis Presley records that kept coming out from the jukebox did, in fact, make a very melodic musical background to the psychic reading, particularly when the songs 'Crying in the Chapel' and 'Wooden Heart' were played. Unfortunately not, on hearing 'Hound Dog' and 'Don't be Cruel'. At the end of the reading the young lady client, in spite of all the unexpected props in the background, appeared to be very pleased with the content of the physic messages received, and even the baby girl was cooing peacefully at the finish. What an unforgettable experience!

An old female client from the Surrey area came for a psychic reading in the early part of this year (2012), and during the sitting it emerged that an elderly male relative had been behaving in an uncharacteristic way regarding his financial situation. This apparently was causing much concern to family members. His strongly intuitive wife had passed into spirit within the last two years, and my client was hoping that this lady might make her presence felt during the reading to give her some advice as to how to handle her husband's worrying behaviour. I always tell clients that spirit will only come through as and when they can, or when they actually want to, and there have been occasions when a client has been desperate for a message from their loved one(s) but without success.

I never usually disclose information given in a private psychic reading because it is immediately removed from my memory for the privacy of my client, but there have been occasions for some unknown reason, where this has not been the case. This time however, I remember it well.

During this psychic reading both my client and I began to experience a distinctly cold tingly feeling throughout our bodies. Also, the room where we were sitting began to drop in temperature. I could then hear the name of a lady being called out and she then began to ask me to relate certain information to my client for several minutes. I also felt that she was indeed a strong spiritual energy. She had advised me of her Christian name, and on relating this to my client I learnt that this had been the wife's name of the elderly male relative who had been causing so much concern. I later was told that she had been an extremely powerful lady whilst on the Earth plane and could read people easily. It appeared obvious to me that she too was concerned at how her husband had been behaving on the Earth plane and had perhaps paid a visit to give her wifely advice.

On another occasion, a very kind and sincere Austrian lady, whom I had met on a crystals course, phoned for a psychic reading. She lived just off Richmond Park and was the wife of a diplomat temporarily based in the United Kingdom. The reading was to be given near her home and we met in Richmond Park in a well-known cafe. Upon meeting we walked a short distance through the park and found am empty long, wooden bench with chairs scattered around and surrounded by shady trees, many of which were of the Oak and Elm variety. We sat down and after a brief explanation of how I worked, a little relaxing meditation followed and then 'tuning in'. I proceeded with the psychic reading, beginning with the client's past through to her present day environment, finishing with events that were to come along her future pathway for even further insight of her life.

I laid the tarot cards out in a variety of spreads. However, halfway through this the pitter-patter of raindrops began to fall onto the leafy trees around us. Fortunately, this also enhanced the elemental aspect of the reading as water elementals can be found wherever water exists, whether in lakes, rivers, the sea or in raindrops (which I will mention a little later on).

Thankfully, the trees surrounding my client and I acted as a huge umbrella for us and the reading continued to flow along. In fact, (without meaning to sound egotistical) so well that the lady concerned wrote to me several months later after she had returned to her home in Austria stating, "I will never, ever forget such a unique psychic reading!"

There are many nature spirits which belong to the Angel hierarchy attached to our lovely trees, bushes, shrubs and flowers, and these particular spiritual energies can also be found in rocks, stones, as well as deep within the earth. Every tree has a spiritual energy of its own which can, in fact, leave the tree for a short while (but not too far away); usually at night time, as during the day the spirit usually helps it to grow more.

Tree spirits are usually strong, and can also be quite loving to us humans, and many people seem to have a particular favourite tree that they gain strength and comfort from on close contact with it. Sometimes we have to be careful when chopping down or trimming unwanted shrubs as many nature spirits have their homes within the shrubs, and it is often difficult later to get anything else to grow in those particular areas where shrubs have been cut down or trimmed.

The Elder tree has many nature spirit energies attached to it and acts as a shelter and protection against other not-so-friendly spirits.

The Oak tree dislikes intensely being cut down, and also the Elm tree feels great sorrow at being disturbed in any way.

The Hawthorn tree is thought by many people to be a fairy tree, and chopping down this particular tree is thought to bring bad luck.

Children often see nature spirits, as these particular spiritual energies like to be around lively and happy homes.

Within the elements of earth, water, fire and air there is an Elemental hierarchy; these energies are of differing shapes and sizes, and they are, namely:

Gnomes are earth elementals, and they work in helping trees, plants and flowers to grow; they help us physically with any bodily abuse, either to ourselves, or from another.

Undines are water elementals, and they often work on us while we are dreaming, thereby stimulating our creative, emotional and nature sides; they also help us physically with our lymphatic system, assisting in the healing of our bodies.

Salamanders are fire elementals and they are active in volcanoes, explosions and lightning, as well as underground; they help us physically with our circulation and metabolism, also our spiritual evolvement. Heat and flames are naturally to do with the salamanders.

Sylphs are air elementals and they help to protect our homes, often by deterring any would-be intruders.

For those of you who may be interested in an astrological aspect to the elements, I have given a short description below:

Earth is connected to the zodiacal signs and symbols of: Taurus (the Bull), Virgo (the Virgin) and Capricorn (the Goat).

Water is connected to the zodiacal signs and symbols of: Pisces (the Fish), Cancer (the Crab) and Scorpio (the

Scorpion).

Air is connected to the zodiacal signs and symbols of: Gemini (the Twins), Libra (Balance), and Aquarius (the Water-bearer).

Fire is connected to the zodiacal signs and symbols of: Aries (the Ram), Leo (the Lion) and Sagittarius (the Archer).

The fifth element, which I have not mentioned above, is Ether which permeates the whole of the Universe and its creation.

I am sure that many of you will have more of an in-depth knowledge than I relating to the vast subject of astrology, but the above is only a brief outline of the elemental connections to astrology, and I will leave it up to you as to whether you wish to gather more knowledge on this particular celestial field.

As I mentioned earlier, I do not usually speak about the contents of the psychic readings given as I have always believed that the information given is both personal and private to the person concerned. In many cases much of it, strangely enough, is removed soon after from my memory. However, there is one particular psychic reading that I gave which unusually does appear to have stayed in my memory - perhaps because of the deep sorrow felt by the lady in question.

I always hope that the information imparted to a client will be helpful, uplifting and a guide as to his or her future direction, but there was a particularly beautiful young lady with long, flowing, dark hair, deep brown eyes, and a porcelain complexion, who came to my house for a reading one autumn afternoon.

She had met a young foreign gentleman, who just happened to be a genuine millionaire, and the young lady (who came from a respectable middle class local family in Surrey) was introduced suddenly to a life beyond her wildest dreams. She had been invited, along with his many family members, to holiday many times on their fleet of luxury ships around the Mediterranean, and was personally introduced to the young man's immediate family. She had been showered with expensive gifts of jewellery, clothes, paintings etc. and had accepted a proposal of marriage, and showed me an enormous sparkling diamond ring on her finger. However, after a few months, her fiancé had appeared to have become very distant with her and was frequently unavailable where she was concerned. She was naturally in a state of distress sitting in my living room and wanted to know the reason why, adding desperately that all she wanted was to be with him and have his babies.

I proceeded to tune in and discovered, sadly, that the young man's apparent sudden disinterest in her was especially to do with two rather strong, menacing energies close to him who had put much pressure on the young man to literally abandon this girl in spite of the family introductions and the engagement otherwise they would completely disown and disinherit him of everything. I also felt strongly that another young female had been handpicked for him. (The two strong energies were his parents.)

I truly wanted to give this young lady (who by that time had broken down in floods of tears) a positive uplifting reading, but of course I had to inform her of the information that I had psychically picked up, adding that a marriage for her was seen later but not, unfortunately, to the young man concerned.

Since that occasion, many people have come to my door for psychic readings, but that particular young lady never seems to be far from my thoughts. And to this day, I so hope that she has now found the life that she so desperately was seeking – and her twin flame. Your twin flame is your true other half, and you feel as one with each other and content. Whereas you can have many soul mates, which usually are people whom you have known in a previous lifetime and who have possibly been family members or even friends or acquaintances, and there is usually some unfinished business to resolve between you.

Chapter 2

Spiritual Encounters, a Psychic Attachment and the House of Ill-Luck

During my puberty years, I moved with my family from our small cottage in the leafy lane to a semi-detached house at the opposite end of the village, which was a noisier area, bustling with lots of people constantly moving about, either on their way to work or the local bus stops, or out tending their gardens which were full of flowers, trees and vegetable patches in the back garden area. I never actually discovered why we moved from the cottage but for me, even as a young girl, it was quite a contrast to our previous way of life.

Upon arrival at our new house, I can clearly remember my mother and I walking up the narrow front garden to the white painted front door when suddenly the next door neighbour came running out to greet us, exclaiming rather loudly that "unfortunately you are moving into what we call here 'the house of ill luck' because of all the unhappy events that have occurred there over the past years to previous occupants".

My mother did not appear to take much notice of these remarks at the time – perhaps feeling that they might be old wives tales and just tittle-tattle. This incident was soon forgotten, but throughout our family's years of living in this house we could not help but notice the undue amount of tragedies that we suffered whilst living there. These included many shocking illnesses, accidents and losses, which were not the usual amount of life's ups and downs that we all may face at some time in our lives.

Whilst living in the house in question, I personally have appeared to have suffered continuously from never-ending bouts of ill health including undue bouts of pneumonia, bronchitis, sight problems, cancer related scares and a constant unprecedented amount of sorrow relating to partnerships since the age of seventeen.

Also, every single opportunity that came my way, no matter how small, in regard to a "once in a lifetime" chance (both business-wise and emotionally) was always taken away from me. In fact, one of these instances was in regard to a wonderful and unusual post as a psychic/medium. I was invited for an interview at a famous department store in Knightsbridge, London, which had recently decided to go into the alternative medicine field by employing several specialists in that field, including a tarot reader, reflexologist, a psychic/medium and various other alternative medicine practitioners. Upon arrival at the store, I was led up to the fifth floor by a lady in charge of their amazing Beauty Department, and after a brief interview about my particular field of work, she informed me that I was to give two psychic readings, one of whom was a Managing Director of the store. I then was taken to a small beautifully furnished room with oil paintings on the wall and thick pile beige carpets and left there for fifteen minutes during which time I tuned into my guide and psychic side in preparation for the forthcoming psychic readings.

After what seemed like an age, the door burst open and in walked an immaculately dressed lady in a royal blue suit, white blouse, royal high heeled shoes, the most amazing icy blue eyes that I have ever seen, and a perfect blonde coiffure on her head, which didn't seem to move one inch! She then just sat down, crossed her long slender legs, peered at me with her icy blue eyes and stated, "I don't believe a word of this, but just read for me now!"

After sending up a quiet call again to my Spiritual Guide, I then proceeded to explain to her how I worked and started with a brief meditation and protection and grounding for both her benefit and mine – all this after both of us had closed our eyes and relaxed for a few minutes. Then, on opening our eyes, I proceeded to read for her which strangely enough delved into her background in the East End of London where her family ran a bakery near Hackney. I was also shown one of her previous incarnations, and later tuned into her present day life and property ventures, also being given a specific health problem which she had suffered from as a child.

All through the aforementioned psychic reading, the lady never uttered one word. However, when her reading was finished, after nearly two hours, she just stood up and said, "That was amazing. You've changed my mind about all this. Welcome on board." She then shook my hand and took me out of the room, introduced me to several members of staff, and said that there would be many famous clients to read for. I was later taken to several of their alternative medicine rooms, including one particular room that took my breath away which was made entirely of pure crystal from top to bottom!

Negotiations for my starting date at the store continued over the next three months and I received several phone calls of encouragement. Then suddenly all contact between the store and me abruptly stopped and I later heard that they had decided to merge their Alternative Medicine business with another famous store in Oxford Street and use this particular store's resident psychic staff. What a disappointment after everything that had happened! (Another instance, perhaps, of "the house of ill luck" – who knows - but at least this was a memorable encounter which I will never forget!)

Over the years all the ill luck incurred by my family and me became so noticeable that we did start to wonder if perhaps our next door neighbour's remark about "the house of ill luck" could have some semblance of truth and my parents endeavoured to find out about the previous occupants in the house.

After much detective work involving asking several older resident neighbours we discovered with some dismay that several tragic events had indeed occurred to the previous occupants of our house, including a little girl who had horrifyingly been burnt to death in the house and an old lady dressmaker had also died there. Strangely enough, my elder brother, Bob, as a young boy could often hear the sound of scissors clicking whenever he was in the lower front room of the house and was later told by the next door neighbour that the old lady dressmaker had actually passed away in that very room.

In his later years Bob often came to visit me at the house. He had married and was living with his wife Christine and son Robert in Nottingham and came not only to see me but to attend his beloved horseracing meetings at nearby Sandown Park racecourse.

After one particular weekend that my brother came to stay, he strangely encountered an unpleasant spiritual experience. Upon his return home to Nottingham it was noticed, with some alarm, that his back was literally covered in long, deep, red welt marks; very similar to angry looking scratches. There was no reason whatsoever for this strange occurrence but what was even more mysterious was that I had since learned the deep welts had completely vanished of their own accord shortly after, without any medical treatment. We could only assume that perhaps there had been a spiritual entity in my house who had been upset in some way, but we never actually found out why this strange occurrence had happened.

I encountered several spirit sightings and encounters in this same house over the past years, one of which happened to me at the tender age of seventeen. My grandmother Amelia, whom I have previously mentioned as being incredibly psychic, sadly passed into the spirit world after suffering with a painful duodenal stomach ulcer that had burst. My family and I were naturally devastated at her passing, and on the morning of her funeral (or "re-birth" as it is known in spirit), I was just lying on my bed upstairs thinking of her when, startlingly, some extremely bright white lights appeared from nowhere along the inner side of the bedroom door, which reminded me of a cluster of night time stars - but this was around 10.30 am in the morning! The bright lights hovered for just a moment, and then suddenly just totally disappeared. I shouted out for my mother, who was downstairs, and she immediately ran quickly up to me to see what on earth was wrong. Excitedly, I endeavoured to explain to my mother exactly what I had just witnessed, when she just calmly and quietly exclaimed, "Oh, that was probably your Nan, (as us children called her) sending you a shower of stars to let us all know that she is all right." This was a sighting which has remained in my memory throughout my lifetime!

On another occasion, approximately six weeks prior to my late father's death, I can distinctly remember yet another sleepless night because of my on-going insomnia problem. However, for some inexplicable reason, it was a particularly bad bout and so I decided to read a little (my small bedside light often being left switched on for this purpose).

However, after endeavouring to read some chapters of a book on the use of crystals, I happened to glance up and, to my amazement, saw what appeared to be the dark figure of a hooded man standing over me. In fact, he looked just like a monk with his habit surrounding him. I was absolutely terrified but found the strength to loudly shriek out for my father in the other upstairs bedroom, but strangely enough, right at that particular moment, the hooded figure just disappeared completely into the atmosphere.

My father then opened my bedroom door, looking obviously concerned as to what was happening, but after I hurriedly described what I had seen, he merely said that he had often seen the monk peering over him in bed and also once whilst our walking locally in an area called 'The Halfway' near Walton-on-Thames, adding that "he had probably got the wrong bedroom".

Sadly, approximately six weeks later, my father passed into spirit. (I would just mention that only last year, the hooded figure reappeared to me in exactly the same way – hopefully not an early warning for myself.)

Another particularly disturbing spiritual encounter happened a few weeks after my father had passed into the spirit world. One particular night, again suffering from my usual insomnia, I was lying in the front upstairs bedroom in my house (the bedroom, in fact, of my late parents) when during the early hours of that following morning I suddenly felt the bed depress as though someone had sat on it, but on looking around there wasn't anyone there – the bedroom was quite light as it was mid-summer. Several minutes later it felt as though the bed had gone back to its normal position. I then got up and looked all over the house to make sure if every-thing was all right – thankfully, things were fine.

The following night, exactly the same occurrence happened again, but this time as I was lying on my side I felt something grip me tightly around my waist then, after several seconds, the grip loosened. Of course, I was terrified and just lay there for a while unable to move. Again, on rising and looking all over the house, everything was in place. Thankfully, nothing else happened the following few days, and I tried to forget about the incidences.

However, one night during the following week, the same scene happened again and yet again I was tightly gripped around my waist. This time I managed to find the strength to gingerly ask who, or what, it was. I then heard a deep toned voice stating, "I am a friend of Delia Sainsbury" and then, what literally shook me to the core of my being, my right hand was suddenly gripped tightly and then released. I instinctively reached out in an endeavour to find out more when, even more alarmingly, I felt what can only be described as a bony skeletal hand. I quickly pulled away and just lay there in bed absolutely beside myself with fear, when several minutes later the bed appeared to go up, as though someone had just stood up from it and then there seemed to be utter stillness and peace within the room.

I could not understand why these strange phenomena had happened to me, so I literally sent out a prayer to "upstairs" to help in this respect. Two days later a thought was put into my mind of how my late father talked at some point about a family named Sainsbury who lived opposite him during his childhood years. It was a family of six girls and apparently the oldest, who was a friend of my father, had died extremely young in a tragic accident. Whether there was a connection to my Delia Sainsbury incident I shall never know, but it was one spiritual encounter that I will never, ever forget.

Another of my initial spiritual encounters happened one beautiful spring morning when I was just 21 years of age. I had awoken quite early that particular morning to the sound of loud cackling in my bedroom which at first I thought was coming from a family member, and on peering around the room, to my surprise, there was no one there. The sound appeared to get louder, and could only be described as that of an extremely elderly lady. By that time I was sitting bolt upright in bed feeling both startled and curious, and it was then I heard what I can only describe as a high pitched cackling laugh and then the statement, "You will never be happy," and then again the cackling high pitched laugh.

Confirmation of the above occurred two years ago when I went to a visit a well-known healer called Wayne Lee. He absolutely had no prior knowledge of my life, particularly as

I had never laid eyes on him before. He confirmed that there was an energy of a very old hunchbacked lady around me who had a high pitched cackling laugh; he also added that she had had a very unhappy earthly life, and alarmingly she had been attached to my (aura) energy field since the age of 21, as apparently, because I was sensitive it had been very easy for her to attach herself to me. Hence the many years of tragic personal setbacks.

I had also attended a psychic workshop one weekend not long prior to seeing Wayne Lee. This was held at a Psychic School in Kingston-upon-Thames, Surrey, and I and several other people sat in a circle one sunny summer morning, in trepidation at what was to come. No sooner had the tutor introduced herself, when she suddenly announced that there was a negative energy hovering between Marianne (myself) and Nancy. One of the other students then exclaimed that the energy had, in fact, attached itself to Marianne. Of course I became alarmed at learning of this and decided there and then to delve even further into exactly who or what had become attached to me and, most importantly, the reason why!

I had often heard about a highly recommended lady by the name of Maria Burke who not only was a highly qualified nutritionist but who also used an advanced technological type of computer call "Quantum Life". Quite incredibly, it illuminates our surrounding energy field and shows on-screen its colours, any energy attachments, or gaps in the energy field, and alongside this relevant answers to infor-mation required. Also, the most amazing revelations concerning any possible past lives that we may have lived.

I managed to see Maria a few weeks later, and after she had literally wired me up to the computer it quickly gathered much information. It showed my aura, which was a shimmering lilac colour and unfortunately it also depicted four dark jagged shapes (energy attachments) connected to it. There was also wording alongside stating "an imposition of others' energy" and then horrifyingly stating that I had lived a past life in 560 AD, where I had apparently committed a crime, which had involved the taking of a life, and I had been a male. The many unhappy, and at times tragic, occurrences that had been happening throughout my present life were, frighteningly, to do with my previous crime.

After much deep thought that same evening, I realised that I had to, once and for all, do something to somehow not only clear the negative attachment to my energy field (aura), but also lift away the remaining unwanted residual energy lurking in my home.

Several months later, I happened to hear of a well-known medium by the name of Dennis McKenzie, who had helped in the solving of the tragic Soham murders. He had apparently also solved several crimes involving murders in Ireland and had also been attached to a Police Constabulary in assisting with some of their unsolved crimes.

I managed to speak to Mr McKenzie over the telephone some weeks later. He stated that there was some negative energy in my house and around me, in particular the energy of a small girl who had tragically died in the house and had attached herself to my aura. Apparently she had been unable to pass over to the other side and was both alone and very unhappy, and even more alarming was the fact that she had at times been using a type of voodoo energy on me; hence causing a lot of the illnesses and sad events that I have incurred over the past years. Mr McKenzie said he would try to gently encourage the young female energy, who was apparently just reaching puberty, to go to the light and join her parents and family where she would be much loved.

A strange phenomenon occurred in my house whilst I was sitting around the old Oak table in my downstairs front room reading. At around 9.15 pm I felt a huge "whoosh" of what can only be described as extremely joyful energy, then there was a tinge of sadness felt and I knew instinctively that Mr McKenzie had succeeded in encouraging the young girl to cross over to the spirit world where she will, hopefully, be surrounded with the love of her family members that she has been denied for so many years.

Many months later I happened to see an advert for a talk being given by a lady called Mrs Lyn Rose about negative energy clearance from in and around buildings, and the impact residual energy has on people. She was also going to discuss ley line energy, which apparently was her speciality.

I managed to hear Mrs Rose's talk one Saturday afternoon not far from Surbiton in Surrey, in a small hall. She was, indeed, an expert in her field and also showed us many energy clearing devices including dowsing rods, metal conductors, small hammers and white candles. At the end of the afternoon I felt very inspired by what I had heard and gingerly approached Mrs Rose to ask her if she could spare some time in her busy schedule to visit my house. She duly obliged and some weeks later arrived, armed with all the energy clearing devices mentioned.

Mrs Rose firstly went straight out into the back garden of my house, and after a thorough inspection, announced that there were two extremely long ley (or grid) lines extending from the end of my garden travelling towards the house and then one was veering up into the back bedroom (which is where I happen to sleep) which ran out through my house towards a large green area in front of the property. Mrs Rose stated that the energy of the ley lines had, in fact, been affecting my energy field, adding that spirits can actually feed off the ley line energy. Mrs Rose then began to arduously hammer two small metal conductors into exactly where the ley lines began at the rear end of the garden to deflect the energy coming from them.

She then went inside my house and remarked that she had felt that there was much residual energy still there coming from the previous owners of the house as well as from my own family members. She mentioned that I had picked up a lot of this energy as well from many other people coming and going there, including clients that I had done psychic readings for, and that much of this energy was not always the positive kind.

She then remarked that she had encountered the presence of a very old looking lady who was a little like the late Queen Mary facially. She discovered later that this woman was the energy that had attached itself to my aura since I was in my twenties (this of course corresponded exactly with what Mr Wayne Lee had sensed). Mrs Rose then proceeded to help her to go into the light, gently explaining to her that all her loved ones were there and that she would be much happier there than remaining here on the Earth plane. She also added that there would be no restrictions on her coming here to the house to visit whenever she wanted to.

After cleansing all the rooms of the residual energy and dealing with the old lady's spirit by helping her to go into the light, Mrs Rose then lit many white candles and we put them in each room to completely remove any negative energy that still remained. If a white candle is lit and left for as long as possible the candle wax will drizzle down the side of it, usually turning into a grey colour wash which represents the negative energy that was there and which had now cleared. Strangely enough, the back bedroom (where I have often seen spirit sightings) and the small downstairs front hall appeared to have had a great deal of residual energy left there from previous occupiers of the house. Also, much geopathic stress from electro-magnetic energy can be thrown out from a range of equipment such as televisions, radios (even if just switched to stand-by mode), computers, telephones (both mobile and cordless) etc., so perhaps some of these devices at home, together with the ley lines and residual spiritual energy, have in some way contributed to my never-ending insomnia condition. Also, other outside devices such as overhead cables and railway tracks can cause havoc within our bodies because of their huge amount of electro-magnetic radiation.

Several weeks went past and I could feel such a lift in the energy of the house and also in myself and I also didn't feel as sluggish as before. Hopefully, the positive new energy will continue to flow in and around my house and within me, enabling joy and laughter to return and bring a sense of peace.

I also try to remember to cleanse the energy of the house daily by either lighting a sage or rosemary stick and wafting their smoke around each room, just clapping my hands over the room walls or in corners as sound is a strong energy trans-former or even just leaving a small container of sea salt in the middle of each room to zap up any negative energy (remem-bering to throw it away afterwards and not to use it).

Also spraying with a crystal or flower essence such as "Crystal Clear" will clear the energy, both around us and within a property. Crystals can also absorb any negative energy vibrations. Placing smoky quartz or obsidian around a room will clear any negative energy, and placing amber will transform the energy. Also, placing rose quartz and amethyst around a room will bring in loving, protective energy. I also breathe in pure white light, visualising it all over me which is not only a form of protection but also a cleansing light. I try to clear out any clutter that has accumulated in my house, as negative energy also collects in the form of clutter and will prevent the flow of new energy.

Also, apparently, the back living room, which also had part of one of the ley line energy running through it up into the back bedroom, had much unwanted energy which might explain the reason for my constant low mood every time I sat in an armchair in a particular corner of that room and where my cat would also always tend to curl up. (Cats tend to sit where a ley line is, but dogs hate them.)

Mrs Rose also mentioned that there was an underground stream flowing from my back garden underneath the house which was throwing out negative energy and can apparently attract unwanted spiritual energy. She was absolutely correct about the stream as my late father stemmed the flow of water many years previously, and Mrs Rose would not have had any way of knowing this.

Chapter 3

Our Auras, a Personal Psychic Attack and Further Spirit Contact

Some of you reading this book may be aware that the Universe is composed of a swirling energy mass, consisting of particles of protons, electrons, neutrons, molecules, gases and of course gravity; not forgetting the huge array of planets and stars encircling this vast cosmos.

Our own individual electro-magnetic energy field that surrounds us, sometimes called the aura, consists of vibrational layers of coloured energy, each one connecting out to the vast spiritual planes. The aura holds all our thoughts, emotions and memories even from our previous lifetimes and sometimes it can become clogged up with too much negative energy which can then travel into our physical body via our seven central energy centres (the chakras that radiate along our spinal cords, from front to back) resulting in actual physical illness. The aura can actually enlarge in size in very healthy individuals, which is when they are often described as "dynamic" or "outstanding" and it can also diminish in size in weaker individuals.

A brief outline of the coloured energy layers of the aura is given below:

The Etheric first layer has the same structure as the physical body (a template or pattern) and can be seen as a white-blue light. It can extend 2" – 3" beyond the physical body and is connected to the Earth plane.

The Emotional second layer is associated with our feelings and can be seen as either a muddy or clear hue, depending on the feeling that generates from within us. It can extend 3" beyond the physical body and is connected to the lower Astral spiritual plane, which is the level of spirit guides, animals and nature spirits and the plane closest in vibration to Earth and where our soul travels to once our Earthly journey is finished, before progressing onto the higher spiritual plane.

The Mental third layer is associated with our emotions, thoughts and ideas and can be seen as a bright yellow colour. It can extend 8" beyond the physical body and is connected to the Rainbow spiritual plane, which is the level of our ancestors.

The Higher Astral fourth layer is associated with our feelings of love and acts as a bridge between the lower and higher spiritual layers. It can be seen as a rose pink colour and can extend 12" beyond the physical body and is connected to the Buddhic spiritual plane, which is the level of Angels.

The Etheric fifth layer is the spiritual template for the lower Etheric and is associated with divine will. When in balance, you yourself will feel both balanced and at one with life. It can be seen as a blue colour and can extend 24" beyond the physical body and is connected to the Atmic spiritual plane, which is the level of Archangels and saints.

The Celestial sixth layer is the spiritual body associated with divine love and bliss. It can be seen as an indigo colour, and can extend 33" beyond the physical body and is connected to the level of deities and the highest Angel levels.

The Ketheric seventh layer is the spiritual template associated with divine mind and, when in balance, you will feel part of this Earthly life. It is also called the Casual body. It can extend 42" beyond the physical body and is connected to the Adi level of God.

I can clearly remember attending a workshop on the Fairy Kingdom at a Mind, Body and Spirit Festival at Kempton Park several years ago when, having arrived a little late, I sat at the rear of the workshop so as not to disturb anyone.

After several minutes, I happened to glance towards the front row of people and was amazed to see vivid bright white jagged outlines surrounding their heads and shoulders, which I knew to be the etheric layers of their auras.

Some were incredibly bright and extremely wide whilst others appeared narrower and a little paler, but still an incredible sight. Of course, I became so entranced at watching all these auras darting about that my concentration on the information about the Fairy Kingdom wavered somewhat.

Another memorable sighting of a particularly beautiful aura appeared whilst I was attending a psychic workshop at the Aetherius Society in Parsons Green, near Fulham, given by a well-known lady called Becky Walsh. Her talk about her psychic experiences was fascinating and I know she has helped many people along her life pathway. Midway through her talk, I was startled to see one of the most unique shades of pale green extending around her head and shoulders which grew to a remarkable width. The heart chakra consists of this colour as well as pink shade, so Becky was perhaps radiating much sincere love out towards the audience at the workshops; again, another incredible sighting.

During the month of October in 2011, I was invited to Nottingham to share in a special birthday celebration for my sister-in-law Christine at a pretty little cafe in the city centre one lunchtime. A party of her closest girlfriends had gathered there, and we tucked into delicious Panini, salads, sandwiches and puddings, amidst much laughter and reflection of years gone by and the memories we had all shared – several being related to their working lives, as several of the ladies had been employed for many years in a government building.

At the close of the celebration Christine, another close friend of hers called Gill and I returned to my sister-in-law's home in Gamston where we made ourselves comfortable on the comfy sofa and armchair. Gill was a friendly, jolly lady who lived in Darlington with her three beloved cats called Phoebe, Dillon and Tabby. As we were discussing the afternoon's events, interspersed with information about our own lives at home, I unexpectedly began to detect directly behind her the emerging outline of a spiritual presence. It continued to form the shape of a smallish medium-built male energy.

As I continued to stare avidly at this astonishing apparition, it started to fade, at which point I quickly shouted to Christine who was busying herself in the kitchen to come and witness what was happening, but alas she was not able to spot the presence. It then slowly began to make itself known again, but this time standing on Gill's left hand side, at which point she hesitantly mentioned that the description matched her late father who had passed to spirit a couple of years earlier. The apparition continued to fade for a few seconds and then re-emerge throughout the rest of the afternoon, during which time Christine sat next to Gill on the sofa in the hope that her late sister would also put in an appearance. But alas it was not to be, which only reinforced my view that spirit will only manifest through the ether either when they want to, or when they are not required elsewhere on the spiritual planes. However, the fascinating, and indeed surprising, visitation of Gill's late father was another truly amazing unexpected and unforgettable sighting.

I have given many psychic readings and one Saturday afternoon last year I happened to be midway through a reading in Ealing for a good friend called Debra, when her aura began to rapidly expand around her showing a truly beautiful pale yellow illumination. Debra had in fact been working hard, particularly on the willpower aspect of her emotions, and this had certainly been depicted in her aura; what a privilege to have seen it.

As mentioned in the earlier part of this chapter, we have several central energy centres (the chakras) that radiate along the spinal cord, from front to back, which connect to the outer aura energy layers. Many of you reading this book will possibly already be aware of the workings of the chakra centres, but for those of you who do not I give below a description of each one, as they play a large part in our spiritual, mental and physical well-being.

The three central lower chakras spin at a slower vibration than the higher centres and are:

The Base (red-coloured) is to do with our Earthly needs and survival as well as grounding and motivation. Its physical links are connected to the adrenal glands, the hips, legs, feet, rectum and spine.

The Sacral (orange coloured) is to do with our sexuality, creativity and change and is situated just below the navel. Its physical links are connected to the reproduction system, the kidneys, the lower back, part of the digestive system and also the gonad gland.

The Solar Plexus (yellow coloured) is to do with our willpower, emotions and self-confidence and is situated above the naval. Its physical links are connected to the stomach, liver, gall bladder and also the pancreas gland.

The Heart (rose-pink or green coloured) is to do with love, compassion and understanding and is situated over the sternum. It acts as a bridge between the lower Earthly chakras and the higher Spiritual chakras. Its physical links are connected to the lungs, chest, arms and upper back.

The Throat (pale blue coloured) is do with all forms of communication and self-expression and its physical links are connected to the nose, ears, back, shoulders inner mouth and thyroid gland.

The Third Eye (indigo coloured) is to do with our intuition, sixth sense and self-reflection and is situated behind the forehead, in between our eyes. Its physical links are connected to the lower brain, vision, ears, nose, throat and pineal gland.

The Crown (violet or white coloured) is to do with our spiritual will and divine enlightenment and is situated at the top of the head. Its physical links are connected to the upper brain and pituitary gland. Halos radiate the purest of love and they are often reflected in religious paintings as exceedingly bright auras.

There are now believed to be several more chakras outside our physical body within our auric field. These are as follows:

The Transpersonal Point is situated a short distance above the inner Crown chakra, and is believed to house our Higher Self (our spirit) which is the part of us that lives beyond our physical Earthly existence.

The Alter Major is situated at the nape of the neck and runs around the nose. It helps us to connect more with our intuition and so is important when doing any kind of psychic work.

The Thyme is situated between the inner heart chakra and inner throat chakra helps to regulate the immune system.

The Hara is situated between the inner solar plexus and the sacral chakra and has a powerful healing capacity, which is why there are many healers who work with this particular chakra.

I will finish by mentioning a little about 21 minor energy chakra centres within our physical body and many even smaller chakras which connect via meridians (energy pathways). They are particularly important in Chinese medicine when acupuncture is given, as there are apparently over two hundred meridians criss-crossing over each of the seven central chakra centres. The meridians relate to individual Yin (female) organs and also Yang (male) organs.

There are two important meridians which are called the Governing meridian and the Conception meridian, and both need to be in balance for good health and intuitive ability to flow. Firstly, there is the Governing energy pathway which starts at the perineum and runs up the back, moving over the top of the head and carries on down to the inner mouth-roof, ending on the outer central upper lip. Secondly, there is the Conception meridian which starts at the perineum, moves up the front of the body and carries on to the inner tip of the tongue, a little below the outer lip. A circuit of energy can be created between these two meridians by massaging the perineum point, whilst at the same time putting the tip of your tongue just behind the front teeth – this will also help to stimulate intuition.

Another energy circuit involves Yuzhen points which are used in a form of healing called Acupressure using a finger massage on certain Chinese acupuncture points that will also stimulate intuition.

Originally, our meridians were all connected to the grid lines that encircle our Earth plane. These lines are now known more as ley lines and they are also connected to a vast grid of universal energy. Over time, our bodies have become disconnected from the ley lines.

During the past two years, I discovered that I had unfortunately been on the receiving end of a particularly unpleasant psychic attack which can occur when another person thinks extremely negatively about you, perhaps when they are angry, jealous or even hate you in some way and automatically a thought form is created from those particular feelings.

Psychic attacks can attract all manner of harshly unpleasant events happening to a person such as on-going illness, work problems, accidents (not just to them, but to close ones including partners, animals etc.), constant sadness, life in general working against them etc. It is important to be careful of our own thoughts as well, so always cancel out a negative thought towards someone by imagining them surrounded in a bubble of pure white light and catch that thought, which will dissolve it, and then think renewed thoughts of forgiveness to you and the other person concerned.

A psychic attack can occur if your aura (energy field) becomes weakened and has holes in it, thus allowing unwanted energies in further. A physical injury or some kind of mental trauma can create a tear in our energy field, or even using drugs or a poor diet can contribute to this.

Also, sometimes black magic such as using voodoo (dolls) is used in a psychic attack, which is one of the most dangerous types of attack. This, unfortunately, was used towards me (as mentioned in Chapter 2), so protecting ourselves daily is extremely important. The easiest way is to either breathe white light all around yourself or imagine a circle of mirrors attached to you facing outwards, which will deflect any negative energy directed towards you. Carrying a crystal or even wearing one, such as black tourmaline, smoky quartz or amber will also help to protect you.

After a chain of numerous on-going personal negative happenings, I decided to visit two extremely gifted psychic healers in the London area to endeavour to get to the root of all the unpleasant occurrences. Strangely enough, both of the psychic healers confirmed separately that I had suffered a serious psychic attack and had seen a large jagged shaped tear in my aura. They even startlingly both stated the name of the person who had psychically attacked me. It was a female, who apparently was an extremely powerful energy herself. Jealousy towards me had been her motive for the psychic attack. I would strenuously like to reiterate that the protection methods mentioned are so important on a daily basis and even more so should you have a strong gut feeling that you may be in the presence of someone who could be directing any negativity towards you.

Our physical and subtle energy bodies are attached by a

silver energy cord, and this can be seen at times by those of us who have found ourselves suddenly out of our physical bodies. Usually this can happen whilst sleeping, meditating or even after going through a trauma and when people often discover themselves floating high above their physical body or in completely different surroundings. This is called an Out Of Body Experience or an O.O.B.E.

Near Death Experiences (N.D.E) are also when a person leaves their physical body, but usually find themselves moving towards a tunnel, which appears to have a bright light at the end of it. Often there are many souls there, some familiar to that person, who encourage him or her to return to their physical, earthly body.

I can remember some years ago a female friend of mine whose aunt had been admitted to a local hospital in Surrey after having suffered with heart trouble. Whilst in the operating theatre, her aunt had clinically 'died' for a short time but was, thankfully and surprisingly, revived. Upon being returned to the hospital ward she told all the staff concerned that she had felt herself literally floating upwards toward the theatre ceiling and was able to watch the doctors and nursing staff work on her physical body below and could hear everything that they were saying. This is, in fact, quite remarkable as I believe that the lady in question had not believed in any form of an after-life whatsoever prior to this happening.

There is one outstanding psychic encounter that will always remain in my memory, as it involved my late mother. One autumn night three years ago, whilst endeavouring to get some sleep in my bedroom, I suddenly felt myself literally leaving my physical body and floating towards the bedroom door and then down the stairs into the front living room. I was both startled and joyous to see my late mother sitting on the sofa – looking as though she were in her forties – together with another slightly older looking lady whom I did not recognise. I remember floating straight towards my late mother and trying to hug her only to feel as though my hands were not holding anything at all! My mother just sat staring ahead of her. I then started to tell her how much I had missed her and loved her, but she continued to just sit motionless looking ahead; the other lady was also sitting in the same way as my mother, not speaking. I also vividly remember that the whole room appeared to be lit up in a bright white light.

After what seemed like a few minutes, I reluctantly said goodbye to my mother and, again, there was no response from her. I then felt myself float out of the room and up the stairs back into my bedroom onto the bed when I felt a slight jolt and I could feel myself back in my physical body. I am not sure that I would like to experience an O.O.B.E on a regular basis but I have been told to carry a shiny black hematite crystal, as it is very grounding and will help me to remain within my body should an O.O.B.E occur again. Also, an angelite crystal will intensify the hematite and give further protection.

Another memorable, but quite alarming, O.O.B.E happened last year when having left my physical body one night and just floated into a small bungalow in a completely different area to where I lived. I found myself going into a small bedroom which had a long window on the left side of a bed in the centre of the room, draped by heavy curtains. I seemed to hover above the bed when a frightening scenario started. Two male figures came into the room and started to ransack it (obviously burglars). Even more petrifying was the fact that one of the men was holding a small gun. I really cannot explain what happened then but suddenly the men appeared to realise that I was there and the man with the gun turned to me, pointing it directly towards me. Right at that point I felt a jolt and found myself back in my physical body in my own house, but absolutely shaking with fear.

To this very day, I cannot fathom out what had happened to me – why I was there – had I floated somewhere by mistake? How had the two men physically seen me if it was my subtle energy body that was in that bungalow room? Perhaps I had visited the lower astral energy plane where I could have inadvertently encountered some unpleasant entities. I think the lesson here for me is to remember to protect myself daily by another simple method of just surrounding myself with white light and affirm loudly that "only spirits in the name of love and light be around me".

I would like to share with you another extraordinary out of body experience, which happened in the early morning hours of a May time night this year. As I previously mentioned, insomnia has relentlessly plagued me throughout my lifetime, and the night in question was no exception. I was still awake at around the 3 a.m. according to my bedside alarm clock and in an attempt to get a little rest I decided to try some meditation – perhaps reaching the 'alpha' consciousness mind-state – who knows! Surprisingly, I managed to achieve my goal in a relatively short space of time, only to then find myself leaving my horizontal physical body and floating out of my bedroom, down the stairs and into the kitchen-cum-dining room vicinity, where the whole area appeared to be bathed in a type of eventide light. I peered into the dining-room and, to my astonishment, I remember seeing very clearly two small children aged about six or seven years old playing boisterously together; they both had short black hair and the little girl had a 'bobbed' hairstyle with a tiny fringe. Although the children continued to be happily dancing around together, there was no sound coming from them, but this was not surprising to me as I understand that the spirit realm's way of communicating is through telepathy.

I then looked in the kitchen and in front of me I noticed three women perched on small chairs communicating quite closely, with the lady in the centre leaning over to her right immersed in some type of conversation. I endeavoured to get a closer look at her when she suddenly looked up at me and to my sheer joy I recognised my late mother who had passed to spirit 25 years earlier from Alzheimer's disease. The look of pure love on my mother's face at her recognition of me is something that will forever remain in my memory, together with the comforting knowledge that all traces of the Alzheimer's condition, which had wreaked havoc on her physical body, having seemingly been erased. And she did, in fact, look much younger than her later years whilst on the Earth plane.

I continued to just stare intently at my mother and I began to experience deeply the love radiating from her. I then went towards her to give her a hug when suddenly the lady on the right of my mother outstretched her hand to deter me. I then clearly recall attempting to push it away when I found my own hand literally passing straight through hers, and suddenly I felt a jolt and found myself upstairs in my bedroom again laying horizontally on the bed wide awake, noticing the time at 3.15 pm. This was undoubtedly an O.O.B.E that will remain with me until the end of my days.

A very vivid spiritual sighting occurred to me several years ago which will always remain in my memory. Several years ago, late one autumn evening, I was preparing to for bed in the hope of trying to get a few hours sleep, as my insomnia seemed to be getting worse. Strangely enough I actually did doze off in the early hours of the morning, but was inexplicably awoken shortly after. My bedroom wasn't quite in total darkness as I had omitted to close the curtains properly, leaving shafts of light coming through the windows. On briefly looking wearily around the room, I was shaken to the core to see two eerie-looking figures standing in the left-hand corner at the bottom of my large double bed. Naturally, I was immediately very frightened indeed ("petrified" is more the word) and just lay there frozen with fear thinking that burglars had entered the house. I then managed to gingerly look more closely at the figures and to my amazement recognised one of them to be my sister-in-law's father who had passed into spirit some years earlier. I also could make out that he appeared to be wearing a brownish coloured dogtooth patterned jacket and grey trousers, and he was staring very intently at me. However, I was unable to make out who the other figure was, standing just behind him. My sister-in-law's father just seemed to stare at me penetratingly for a couple of seconds at which point I let out one almighty scream and shouted for help. In that instant, both figures just vanished into the atmosphere.

After a few minutes of just lying there unable to move, I finally managed to slowly leave my bed and go nervously all round my house looking in every nook and cranny for signs of a possible break-in but, after a thorough search, everything appeared to be intact. For the rest of that morning, and in fact for quite some time afterwards, I was still in shock from such a traumatic experience and often find myself relating what had happened to family and friends, who cannot fathom out why I had had the pleasure of such a nerve-racking spiritual sighting!

Another spiritual encounter happened two years ago in the early hours one springtime morning. I had dozed off a few hours earlier after a particularly restless night, only to be awoken by not only the sound of birds twittering away outside my bedroom windows, but also by an inexplicable sense of something hovering over me.

As I slowly began to open my eyes more fully, I was shaken to the core, as standing close to me on the right hand side of my bed was a male figure whom appeared to be dressed in light coloured shorts and shirt, and unbelievably, a wide brimmed hat with what looked like tassels dangling all around it.

He reminded me of an Australian bushman. He just stood there in the early morning light appearing to look literally straight through my horizontal figure laying in the bed, then just completely disappeared into the atmosphere. As you can imagine, it was quite some time before I got the strength to actually start to get myself together and go downstairs for a reviving cup of tea. Again, I still don't know the reason for this spiritual entity coming to pay me a visit and perhaps I shall never discover the answer.

Chapter 4

An Outstanding Angel Sighting, Déjà Vu Evidence of Animal Spirits and a Pathologist's Spiritual Sighting

There are seven Archangels who work on our Earth plane, along with a great multitude of other Archangels amidst the vast Universe; namely:

Archangel Gabriel who is the Angel of the South; she will bring hope, justice, inspiration, creativity and intuition, and her element is water. Archangel Gabriel's day is Monday and the colour associated with her is white. (I am sure some readers will notice that I have gone against the grain and referred to Gabriel as female. This is because I believe Gabriel to be androgynous and his/her feminine side resonates with me the most.)

Archangel Michael is the Angel of the North: he is a protector against harm who will bring motivation, ambition and strength within us and his element is fire. Archangel Michael's days are Sunday and Thursday and the colours associated with him are red and blue.

Archangel Uriel is the Angel of the West: he will bring wisdom, change and tranquillity and his element is earth. Archangel Uriel's days are Tuesday and Friday and the colours associated with him are purple and gold.

Archangel Raphael is the Angel of the East; he is the healing Angel and helps all earthly healers including complementary medicinal healers, doctors and nurses. His element is air and his special days are Wednesday and Saturday and the colour associated with him is emerald green.

Archangel Chamuel assists in all areas of relationships,

including love, conflict and loss. He also helps us to love ourselves unconditionally. His day is Monday and the colour associated with him is pink.

Archangel Zadkiel helps with spiritual growth, understanding, compassion and emotional inner calmness within us. His day is Saturday and the colour associated with him is violet.

Archangel Jophiel brings perception, intuition, wisdom, creativity and he helps in removing negativity. His day is Sunday and the colour associated with him is pale gold.

If you wish to call an Archangel, you can attract them into your life more easily if you invoke them on their special days and also light a candle in the particular colour associated with that Angel. Their love will *never* fail you.

I would like to share a truly memorable Angelic sighting with you which I feel was such a privilege to have witnessed. Many years ago my ex-partner was staying with me one Saturday and during that night I was, yet again, having trouble getting to sleep with my usual insomnia. The bedroom door was slightly ajar and some light was streaming through from my neighbour's upstairs landing light (our houses are very close together) when on looking around the room there was one of the most spectacular and unforgettable visions that I have ever encountered.

Standing just in front of the bedroom door was the figure of an extremely tall robed man with light coloured hair. He looked to be at least seven feet tall, but there was something even more startling, for just around his shoulder area there appeared to be what looked like very small dark wings.

He seemed to just stand and stare directly at me without uttering a word, at which point I turned and endeavoured to wake my partner laying next to me who was sound asleep. However, on turning back and looking towards the door, the vision had just disappeared. I immediately arose and looked all over the upper rooms of my house and then downstairs, but everything was as normal.

I would like to mention, as I am sure many of you reading this will already know, we all have our Spirit Guide and Guardian Angel who are with us when we are born and remain with us when we pass into the Spiritual Realm. We also have a Doorkeeper Guardian who acts as a gatekeeper against anything harmful from the spirit world approaching, so perhaps my Guardian Angel or Doorkeeper had come as a warning to me to be extra vigilant about something.

As previously mentioned, I do firmly believe that a lot of us have lived many lifetimes on the Earth plane, which could be to learn unfinished lessons. There are those of you reading this who have probably visited a particular village, town or even a foreign country who will have experienced a feeling of 'knowing' that area already even though you have never set foot there before. Also, there may be people whom you have encountered and whom you have instantly recognised but have never actually met before. Déjà vu is a term sometimes applied to this unusual phenomenon (which is known as a sensation in our minds of repeating an event that has already taken place).

I strongly feel that déjà vu is connected with our past life incarnations i.e. where we have lived in a particular area or country during a past life on Earth, or known certain individuals during that time and those people, like us, reincarnate here again and cross our paths in order to also learn their unfinished lessons – sometimes with us – or in a different guise and environment.

I can remember staying in a small flat that belonged to a local social club that had been built literally hundreds of years ago, where I was a member for some time. The residents were away on vacation at the time and a friend and I offered to keep an eye on the place. However, upon walking into the flat near the club, I had an extremely uneasy feeling of just wanting to run away from the premises. This feeling stayed with me throughout the whole time we remained there.

Sometime later, I decided to ask a local historian's advice to see if he could shed any light on that particular flat and the surrounding properties. He informed me that during the Oliver Cromwell era in our English history, several hundred Cromwellian troops had actually stayed in the vicinity and many Royalist troops had entered the area where there had, in fact, been a fierce battle resulting in many lost lives. This had actually taken place on the site of the Social Club and the flat nearby where I had stayed. Possibly, therefore, that persistent uneasy feeling I had experienced whilst there and the desire to just get away, was all connected with the residual energy left there. This type of energy can have a marked effect on sensitive individuals, particularly when they live in a property where previously the site has incurred many lost lives, such as a battle area or a burial site such as a churchyard.

One particular karmic encounter which I would like to share with you is when, several years ago, I visited the French walled city of St Malo. It sounded such an unusual place to see, and I felt a strong intuitive urge to go there. Upon my arrival I had a strange feeling of knowing the area, which became even stronger when I took a bus tour of the town. Approximately 10 minutes into the tour, the bus turned into a narrow street where there were white shuttered houses with long front gardens, flowers and long garden paths. On passing one of the houses in the middle of the street I instantly knew that particular house, even knowing that I had lived there as part of a family – being a wife and mother of three small children. The more I looked at the house and surrounding roads, the less I needed a tour guide, as I knew every inch of the area. In fact the more I wandered around other areas during the next two days, the more I came to realise that I had probably lived a previous incarnation there.

Another déjà vu experience happened to me when I decided to go on a guided tour of Hampstead in London. Upon arrival, I walked slowly around the quirky streets and noble-looking properties, including trudging across Hampstead Heath to marvel at the view across London and learning of its history.

However, as I proceeded to trot around the various quaint alleyways and streets, I realised with a jolt that I already knew every inch of the Hampstead area even before setting foot in the place, and I also kept experiencing what can only be termed as a dreadful desire to get away from there as quickly as possible causing my heart to thump rapidly with some terrible sort of fear about the place. I can only assume that I had possibly already lived in Hampstead in a previous incarnation, albeit not very happily, so perhaps I will make an effort to revisit that area to see if I can physically pick up any further lead as to what happened in a possible previous lifetime there.

I sometimes go to short lectures on a Friday morning at a local adult education centre near to my home. One Friday, a particular talk involved 'Literary London in the 18th and 19th Centuries' which described the famous writers and poets of those eras, such as Daniel Defoe (Robinson Crusoe), William Blake (Jerusalem), George Eliot (Middlemarch), Oscar Wilde (The Importance of Being Earnest) and many other geniuses of the day.

There was a slide show given by the Blue Badge London Guide, which depicted several meeting places where the famous literary set would gather in coffeehouses and taverns. One particular tavern called The Trafalgar in Greenwich was shown which was a majestic looking cream coloured building overlooking the river with wrought iron balconies surrounding it. As the slides continued to show more of the tavern, both inside and out, I knew without a shadow of a doubt that I had already been there, although I had never laid eyes on the place before, as I recognised every nook and cranny of the building, including the outer passageways and extensive garden area. I also instinctively knew that I had been a writer during that time.

I later learnt with much interest that literary dinners and soirees were frequently held to celebrate the publication of the novels written by the literary crowd gathered there, so possibly I have reincarnated here on the Earth plane again to finish or learn some lessons connected to this side of life, by way of people or a situation – only time will tell as I continue to discover more and more along my pathway.

I would like to talk a little now about the animal kingdom, in particular our cat fraternity. My family have always tended to have a great regard for all living creatures, including dogs, cats, birds, hedgehogs and even various creepy-crawly spiders often appearing through plugholes at home, which were always encouraged to turn around and return to their own home territory! Although always a little afraid of cats for no fathomable reason, I have had numerous cats of all shapes, sizes and colours venture towards my home absolutely refusing to leave, even going without any home comforts being offered and being firmly chased away.

There was one particularly sad instance when a tortoise-shell cat called Molly whom I had looked after since her young kitten days suddenly, without any apparent warning, passed into the spirit world. This left me devastated as she was more to me than just another cat. She was, in fact, more like a soul mate with her deep, wise, knowing understanding of how I ticked. I always felt that Molly was, indeed, a very old soul on this Earth plane. On the day of her passing, I returned home feeling naturally grief stricken although there was yet another cat called Simpson at home (a large, tubby grey coloured creature who had run away from its owner and headed straight in the direction of my 'animal guest house').

Nothing could stop my tears. I phoned a good friend that evening who was also herself an animal lover and as I sat at the foot of the stairs in the small front hallway crying down the phone line, Simpson (who was such a fearless animal) walked up to me and started to look up towards the middle of the stairs behind me, with her eyes wide open, her ears pricked up and her fur literally standing on end. Then most uncharacteristically, she startlingly leapt behind the stair banister, peeping gingerly upwards toward the same spot midway on the stairs and then back towards me as though endeavouring to share with me what she appeared to be watching. Simpson then timidly ventured out and tried to walk past me up the stairs, only to hurriedly run back yet again behind the banister, eyes wide open, her fur standing on end. At that point, I felt very strongly that there was some sort of a spiritual entity around the particular area concerned and I just turned around and spoke quietly to whom it was; perhaps it was Molly – only Simpson will ever know that answer though.

Personally, I feel that one of the most convincing pieces of evidence for a spiritual animal kingdom came to me by way of an old affectionate black cat named Reg. His owners had looked after him well for nearly eleven years, when Reg inexplicably decided himself to change his residence and found his own way to my 'animal guesthouse' – even after much cajoling to return home to his rightful owners. He was an old soul, and physically long-backed and very bony, being of advancing years. He had survived many of life's knocks, one of them having been a car smash involvement, in which he had broken his jaw, had teeth knocked out and had to be drip-fed for many months – only to bounce back with great tenacity and making an astounding recovery. I cared for Reg as best I could, giving him much love and attention. One sunny spring morning, for no apparent reason, something prompted me to grab my old fashioned camera and take a few photographs of him while he was sitting quietly alone on the lawn in my back garden. Reg obligingly stared at the camera lens and I clicked away taking the photos, taking advantage of the beautiful calm spring day.

Several days later, whilst in the Wimbledon area, I took the film for development. However, when I returned to the shop to collect the developed film, I was inexplicably ushered aside by the gentleman who had developed the photos who then began to ask me many questions about the cat (Reg) in the photos. He explained that whilst developing the film, he had experienced an icy cold feeling around him and had had a pins and needles sensation all though his arms. When I myself glanced at the photos I was shocked, as draped across Reg's old back was a strange looking young creature with grey coloured fur. Reg was so thin and weak that he was incapable of carrying anything, let alone another animal on his poor old back. There also appeared to be another cat's long tail positioned over his head and what looked like a cat's claw on his right side. I would reiterate that there was definitely only Reg and I in the garden at that time, and I did not see any other animals anywhere near him during or after the photo-shoot.

Two weeks later poor old Reg, without any prior warning, passed into the spirit world, so perhaps there had already been some spirit animals gathering, as seen in the photos, in preparation for his departure. Some days later I contacted a well-known psychic and good friend called Mrs Shirley Jones and after sending her the photos she sensed also that the animal spirits around Reg were helping him to prepare for his passing into spirit. One of the photos is shown for you all to perhaps draw your own conclusions on this inexplicable occurrence.

Not long after Reg's passing I was of course still very upset, so one evening I stood at home in front of a large coloured painting of my Spiritual Guide, 'Jake', (a spiritual artist painter called Patrick Gamble had depicted my Guide, hence the painting, whom I had already psychically seen myself prior to his painting) howling with grief at Reg's passing. After several long minutes, I sobbingly asked my Spirit Guide if Reg was all right in spirit – at which point there was what I can only describe as a very unexpected sharp prod in the middle of my back. I instantly whirled around to see what it was only to discover that there was no one there. This left me in no doubt whatsoever that my guide had come through to reassure me that Reg was indeed alright in the spirit realms. How loving, as always, spirits are and will always try to help us in our hour of need.

When I was developing my psychic side in the early years, I attended a psychic college in Kingston-upon-Thames, Surrey. During that time there happened to be an elderly gentleman attending the psychic courses who had been employed as a pathologist in a London government department. In fact, he had apparently gradually climbed up the ladder of success in the 30 years that he had worked there, eventually becoming Head of the Pathology Department. The reason that he was attending the Psychic College, he told us, was because of the inexplicable events that he and his staff had witnessed during that time.

The particular circumstances concerned had, he commented, both intrigued and unnerved him, and he wanted to find out more about a possible after-life. He added that his work had involved working on the many corpses that were brought in to endeavour to confirm the exact cause of death, etc. He and his staff had, apparently, always observed an inexplicable sighting within three days of a corpse being brought into their pathology department for examination, which was a mysterious large puff of white smoke arising from the body and up into the atmosphere. He had reported this sighting many times to his superior officer, but was told every time not to mention this to anyone outside of the Pathology Department.

Another strange sighting he described which had particularly unnerved him was after he had been working on the corpse of a young female who had been brought into the department after a car crash. After working on the body late that evening, he was driving home and after approximately twenty minutes he felt an unusually icy cold atmosphere. He happened to look into the rear view mirror of his car when, to his amazement, he saw the young girl concerned sitting in the back seat in exactly the same clothing that she had been wearing when first brought into his department and she had a faint smile on her face. Naturally, he was very shocked and extremely shaken by this and just managed to pull the car into a nearby lay-by where he sat for over an hour just trying to compose himself. However, on forcing himself to look again into the rear view mirror, the woman had mysteriously vanished. He stated that this incident would stay with him forever and it was not long after this inexplicable event that he wanted to find out more about a possible spiritual after-life and started to attend the psychic college mentioned above.

Chapter 5

The Never Failing Love, Protection and Care of the Spiritual and Angelic Realms

I have always felt that spirits always try to protect, care and forewarn us of a situation that may cause us pain and suffering. This was particularly relevant just before Molly my devoted tortoiseshell cat passed into the spirit as, for two weeks beforehand I kept finding numerous small, white plastic crosses at my feet wherever I happened to walk. Also, one particular autumn afternoon, there appeared to be more than usual of these white crosses as I was walking near my home. I also happened to look up at the unusually clear blue sky when immediately above my house was a large white cross; Molly crossed over into the spirit world very soon after!

Another instance of spiritual protection was when I had been working in America in my early twenties and had met a man who was an artist. We dated several times and we had some wonderful days out in New York, often just walking around the city or going to local clubs in the evenings. He was a perfect gentleman, always looking after me, and giving me many compliments.

However, on one particular occasion after he had invited me around to his studio to see his drawings and paintings, things took an exceptionally unexpected turn for the worse, as he suddenly seemed to more and more become a completely different character – shouting obscenities at me and suddenly pacing quickly about the studio and then turning towards me stating that he was going to physically assault me – with a knife held in his hand! I was, of course, absolutely petrified and just froze on the spot but managed to scream out loudly for help. There was nobody around or near his studio, and I stood there, helpless, thinking that this was going to be my last moment on Earth. I screamed even louder, shouting that "if there was a God then please help me as I didn't want to die".

Exactly at that moment, something made me reach out to my right in the small sparse studio, just strewn with artwork everywhere, and I felt a blunt heavy object at my side. Instinctively I picked it up as the man was approaching me armed with a knife and with unbelievable unexplainable strength I hit him with the object at the side of his head at which point he staggered, appearing to momentarily be very dazed and disbelieving of what had happened. At that moment I managed to get to the studio door, fling it open and get away from there as quickly as possible. I happened to look back, only to see that he had recovered his senses and appeared to be chasing slowly after me. I managed to hail a taxi (which was very unusual, as taxis were never available when needed) and finally got home and literally fell into the arms of my flatmates. I was given a very stern talking to that New York was a dangerous city and I should never have visited that studio with him and to trust on-one there. After much dilemma and thought, of course their warning was so true, but I firmly feel that the spiritual world had stepped in to protect me in my true hour of need and also, with hindsight, I believe that it was not my time to cross over to spirit at that particular time.

Another loving example of spirits' care and concern happened to me one Christmas Eve seven years ago. I often visited a local social club – more to listen to the excellent bands who played there – strumming away to the sounds of the 1950's, 1960's and 1970's, with Elvis, Cliff and The Searchers being their red-hot favourite artists to imitate.

On the Christmas Eve mentioned everyone, including

myself, was on top form dancing and singing along to the sounds of the 60's, after which a huge festive raffle had been organised. Many of us had purchased numerous weekly tickets for the past three months as the prizes often included televisions, computers, household goods and enormous food hampers. I was never lucky, unfortunately, at winning much at all whenever the past year's raffles had been held, so I didn't really pay much attention whenever the winning tickets were announced.

That particular Christmas Eve, for some unfathomable reason, I could distinctly feel an overwhelming sensation of loving energy surrounding me all evening and I kept sensing my late mother with me. Also, I was feeling particularly buoyant as everything during that year had been going really well for me health-wise, financially and socially – as various new people had unexpectedly come into my life – mainly connected to the psychic world, including crystal healers and tarot readers – 'right up my street'!

As the Christmas raffle got underway and the assorted prizes were distributed, suddenly my name was read out along with the unexpected announcement that I had won one of the huge Christmas hampers which not only included the usual festive fare of tinned meats, fruits, Christmas puddings, mince pies, wine, and the finest Scotch whisky, but there was also, on inspection of this massive hamper, enough food and drink produce to last me for the next two months. A friend helped me to get the hamper to my home and I quickly said a silent prayer for my good fortune.

Totally unexpectedly however, five days later, I became very ill with an extremely worrying bout of pneumonia and, living alone at that time, the huge food hamper was a blessing in disguise to say the least, as all the food that I would later need was already at my fingertips, without any worry of having to do any food shopping for weeks to come! Perhaps spirits, in their constantly loving and protective way, had seen what was about to happen to me and had decided to send a loving and caring hand.

I have noticed on more than one occasion, that Earth Angels have appeared physically to have a somewhat unusual aspect to their appearance. Sometime ago there was an exceptionally distressing child abuse case, which was publicised in the National Press for many months. I myself tended to be deeply disturbed at what the poor baby had suffered and, like many others, decided one weekday to pay a visit to the London cemetery to lay flowers and pay my respects for all the suffering endured by the poor little mite concerned. On arrival at the cemetery, I was amazed at just how vast it was and was just like a town. I later learnt that it is actually one of the largest cemeteries in the United Kingdom.

I duly started to proceed to follow the directions of a security guard at one of the entry gates, and thereafter seemed to be endlessly walking up and down brightly coloured flower filled walkways and off the beaten track paths, which appeared to just go on and on for miles, at which point I nervously realised that I had become completely lost in the middle of that vast quiet area, without a single soul in sight. I plodded on, becoming more panicky at every unfamiliar new pathway, thinking that I would probably have to camp down and eerily spend the night there as I didn't even have a mobile phone on me, and I said a silent prayer for help. I could not believe my eyes for at that precise moment, a lady appeared out of the blue just ahead of me, smiling and beckoning me to her. As I approached her I noticed that there was something quite unusual about her facial features, as her nose appeared to be unusually up-turned and also there appeared to be a serene smile on her face. As she spoke, there was just a low quiet tone to the few words that she uttered, whilst continuing to beckon me to follow behind her. From then onwards, after

I had endeavoured to explain to her the purpose of my visit, nothing further was said, but the calmness surrounding both myself and this unusual lady was all-consuming. When we finally arrived at the particular grave concerned and I had paid my respects to the poor little child, laying my bunch of pink and yellow flowers amongst the mountain of wreaths and tributes there, I turned to go, only to find the lady standing behind me with the same serene smile on her face beckoning me, once again, to follow her – without uttering a word. What was even stranger was the fact that we appeared to be the only ones there in that vast area at that particular time.

As we finally arrived at one of the main gateways, I looked for a sign to the local rail station but, on turning to thank the lady in question, she had mysteriously vanished from sight. I am utterly convinced, once again, that another 'Earth Angel' appeared in my hour of need.

Another, albeit shorter, incident of an 'Earth Angel' took place after I had been suffering with the after effects of an eye operation last year. One particular afternoon I was on my way into the large, multi-cultural town of Kingston-upon-Thames to do some retail therapy clothes shopping. The bus that I was travelling on began to approach its final destination when I noticed the familiar face of a female passenger entering the bus. The familiarity I quickly realised was because of her unusual up-turned nose and the serene smile on her face. She then appeared to be heading directly towards me, quietly sat by my side, and even more startlingly, turned and stated "Don't worry, I had a similar problem to you, and remember, there is an eye hospital very nearby"! I just stayed there, absolutely speechless, wondering how she could possibly have known about me, when she quickly stood up and signalled to the bus driver to allow her off the vehicle. I am, once again, firmly convinced that spirit had sent another

'Earth Angel' in my hour of need.

We have, of course, our physical body and our subtle energy system within which our spirit is housed, as previously mentioned. Also there are the three energy layers of our mind, that include our all powerful subconscious, where all our memories are stored from lifetime to lifetime, the subconscious mind can also draw all sorts of phenomena towards us. I was finishing writing about my terrifying experience in New York very recently when a prime example occurred of just how powerful our subconscious can be. I would like to share it with you.

I was writing earlier about the horrifying and unforgettable incident in the artist's studio. Also sadly reliving every single moment in my mind, including remembering the evil expression on the face of my attacker. I managed to complete the article and left the coffee shop where I had been writing and slowly sauntered in the direction of my home. It was a quiet starry September night and I had very often walked in the same direction during the past years, as it was an extremely safe area.

However, that particular evening took a peculiar turn for the worse personally for me, as just as I was nearing my house I turned into a nearby close and could not help but notice a large dark coloured car slowly coming to a halt in the middle of the road just in front of me.

As I continued to walk nearer and pass the vehicle, I felt an icy shock run through me for, unbelievably, as I glanced towards the car the driver was the exact replica facially, even with the same evil expression, as my attacker in New York. I hastily darted behind the car and ran down the pathway of a nearby house that thankfully still had its lighting on and I hid behind some bushes, at which point the man concerned had reversed the car and appeared to be looking in all directions for any sign of me.

I stayed hidden for what seemed like an eternity until finally managing to detect that the coast was clear, I ran as fast as I could in the direction of my home and just sank down indoors in sheer disbelief at just how powerful our thought energy and written words can be in drawing situations, people and events toward us via our subconscious mind. Spirit had not only protected me, but perhaps there was a lesson for us all here to remember to be extra careful about what we negatively dwell on and switch immediately to a more positive frame of mind to counteract any possible unpleasant energy which we may have indirectly drawn towards us.

Another example of how protective and caring spirit can be occurred whilst I was on a short Spanish holiday one Christmastime. I had been invited by my partner of the day to go on a short fun filled cruise, which would include wonderful food, dancing, cabarets and even some time for a shopping trip for a few hours on the Spanish mainland. I had been feeling in need of a break away from my usual surroundings, so jumped at the opportunity of a new environment, albeit only for a few days. The ship was festively decked out with Christmas trees, decorations and twinkling blue and red lights everywhere and we started to get into a festive mood. However, the sea journey was truly shattering as on approaching the Straits of Gibraltar there was a ferocious storm and we were rocking about all over the place, passengers being flung from pillar to post. I managed to make it in one piece back to the cabin, where I was physically unwell for hours thereafter, not being a very good sailor at the best of times.

My partner was physically and mentally the complete opposite of me and it was literally water off a duck's back to him, even appearing to enjoy all the mayhem going on around him! Unfortunately he was unsympathetic to my predicament and from then on proceeded to take every opportunity to distance himself from me. On a later occasion, when the sea was calmer, I endeavoured to venture out and make an effort to enjoy the Christmas festivities, by which time my partner had softened somewhat and he had met a couple of shipmates who invited both of us to join them for the remainder of our time on board.

However, my partner appeared outwardly to behave in a frighteningly uncharacteristic manner towards me, even prompting our friends to ask him to refrain from this sort of attitude towards me, especially in front of company. Throughout our stay, things proceeded to get worse, but spirit must have been there, once again, endeavouring to protect me, as what is called an 'Earth Angel' suddenly appeared in the shape of one of the newly formed friends sitting with us. She was a lady of about 35 years of age and at every opportunity she was there, sometimes even physically standing over me to shield me from whatever unpleasant and hurtful situation arose. Thankfully, this continued until we eventually disembarked, for what had transpired to be a nightmare voyage.

After that trip I never heard from or saw her again, but will always be extremely grateful to this 'Earth Angel' for her great warmth and protection.

I will never, ever forget just how loving, protective and caring the Spiritual and Angelic Realms are, particularly in our times of desperate need and distress. Personally I will always be so humbly grateful to them for the astounding evidence that I have had the good fortune to have witnessed, and do hope that you, yourselves, will be given this same humble privilege before you re-enter the wondrous spiritual planes.

In conclusion, and in memory of my late Father, William John Green, I would like to share with you part of his reflective thoughts written in April 1986:

"I have searched all my life for an answer to the origins of life and have in the end finished up where I started, as though we are never to be allowed to know, always finishing up against a blank wall. The purpose and reason of our being here? As I see it, it would not matter if mankind was swept away without a trace within a moment. This planet Earth would still go on like the others, until its turn for destruction comes. What is the purpose of it all? Man is only a small insignificant part of the whole, no more important in the real make up than a worm. He assumes he is but it is only his ego. The highest and the lowest are equal as in death. We have the same construction as most animals, heart, blood etc., and a limited spell of years. How can we go anywhere else with this body which is constructed for life on this planet? Only if there is a spirit, which survives death and moves freely through space."

6th Books investigates the paranormal, supernatural, explainable or unexplainable. Titles cover everything included within parapsychology: how to, lifestyles, beliefs, myths, theories and memoir.